CRAFT BOX

WORLD WAR II

12 projects to make and do

First published in 2013 by Wayland
Copyright © Wayland 2013

Wayland
338 Euston Road
London NW1 3BH

Wayland Australia
Level 17/207 Kent Street
Sydney, NSW 2000

Editor: Elizabeth Brent
Designer: Rocket Design (East Anglia) Ltd
Craft stylist: Annalees Lim
Photographer: Simon Pask, N1 Studios
Proofreader/indexer: Susie Brooks

The website addresses (URLs) listed in this book are correct at the time
of going to press. However, it is possible that contents or addresses may
have changed since the publication of this book. No responsibility for any
such changes can be accepted by either the author or the Publisher.

Picture acknowledgements:
All step-by-step craft photography: Simon Pask, N1 Studios; images
used throughout for creative graphics: Shutterstock.

A cataloguing record for this title is available at the British Library.
Dewey number: 940.5'3-dc23

ISBN: 978 0 7502 7978 9

10 9 8 7 6 5 4 3 2 1

Printed in China

Wayland is a division of Hachette Children's Books,
an Hachette UK company.
www.hachette.co.uk

Contents

World War II

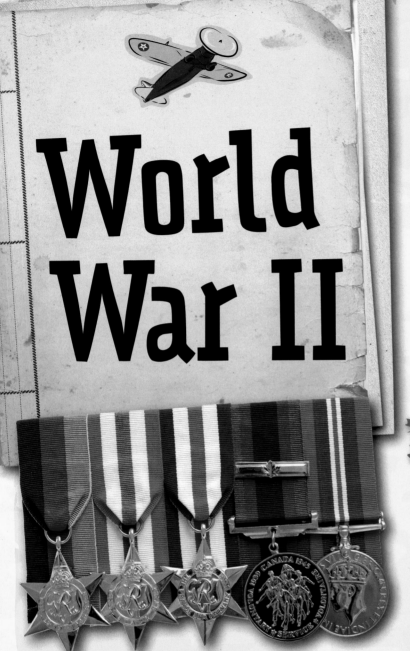

World War II was fought from 1939–1945

World War II began in 1939. It was fought mainly in Europe and Asia between Britain and Germany and their allies. Britain and France declared war on Germany when its leader, Adolf Hitler, sent troops into Poland. Hitler believed that the German race was better than others and should rule other countries.

In Britain, many young men were called up to fight for their country. The war was fought on land, at sea and in the air. During air raids known as 'the Blitz', British cities were attacked by German bomber planes. Many children became evacuees, sent away from their homes to live with families in the countryside to escape the bombing.

Blockades by German ships and submarines meant that food and other goods had to be rationed. People were given coupons to buy their small share of goods such as meat and butter each week. They helped the war effort by 'digging for victory', growing vegetables on every scrap of land, even on the roofs of their bomb shelters. Clothes were rationed too, so families learned to recycle old clothes and other materials so that nothing was wasted.

Around 60 million people, including 40 million civilians, were killed around the world during the war. Many families lost homes and loved ones. But everyone in Britain pulled together, encouraged by radio broadcasts from Prime Minister Winston Churchill. Home crafts and skills became an important way to help the war effort on the Home Front. Be inspired by the wartime spirit and make some wartime crafts of your own.

make a
Gas mask

Poison gas had been used as a weapon during World War I, and people feared that German planes might drop gas bombs on British cities. Gas masks were handed out to all civilians, including children and babies, and people were warned to carry them at all times.

1 Draw the mask shape onto the card and cut it out.

2 Draw around the cardboard tube to mark the nose/mouth and eye holes. Cut them out.

3 Cut the rims away from the transparent lids and glue them behind the eye holes.

4 Cut the cardboard tube down to about 6cm, then snip one edge and flare it out.

5 Cut a circle of bubble wrap and tape it over the other end of the tube. Cover the outside of the tube in black card, then push the flared end through the nose/mouth hole and tape in place.

6 Cut a piece of elastic about 15cm long. Pierce a hole on either side of the mask and push the elastic through, knotting to secure it. Cut a strip of grey card and stick it around the mouthpiece.

Did you know...
Children had to do gas drills and practise putting on their masks in school.

make a
Warden's helmet

Volunteer Air Raid Precautions (ARP) wardens used whistles and sirens to warn people of air raids and get them into shelters. They checked all lights were turned off during the 'blackout' and organized rescue work after raids. They wore badges and helmets so that people could identify them.

1 Turn the bowl upside down and cover it in cling film.

2 To make papier maché, mix equal parts of white glue and water. Dip strips of tissue paper into the glue mix then smooth them onto the cling film. Finish with a layer of kitchen paper, leave to dry then lift off the bowl

3 To make the helmet brim, draw around the papier maché bowl onto some card. Cut around the circle, leaving a 4cm gap all the way round, then cut the circle into triangles.

4

Bend the triangles, and tape them to the inside of the papier maché bowl, so the brim sits around it.

5

Draw a large capital W on one side of the helmet.

6

Paint the helmet black, leaving the letter W white. Go over the letter with white paint.

Did you know...
All lights had to be turned off in a blackout to stop them from guiding in enemy bomber planes.

make a
Doodlebug

Doodlebugs were flying 'V1' bombs that were used by Germany to attack Britain during the war. People knew they had to rush to a bomb shelter when the sound of the V1s' engines died, because it meant the 'buzz bombs' were about to drop.

You will need:

- ◎ Long balloon
- ◎ Balloon pump (optional)
- ◎ White glue and water
- ◎ Tissue paper
- ◎ Kitchen paper
- ◎ Ice cream sticks
- ◎ Scissors
- ◎ Craft stick
- ◎ Small cardboard tube
- ◎ Grey acrylic paint
- ◎ Brushes

1 Blow up a long balloon.

2 To make papier maché, mix equal parts of white glue and water. Dip strips of tissue paper into the glue mix then smooth them onto the balloon, laying them one way then the other way to make a criss-cross pattern. Finish with a layer of kitchen paper and leave to dry.

3

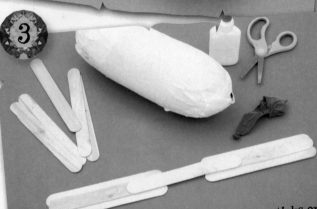

Make the wings by gluing two ice cream sticks on top of one stick. Then glue these wings to another stick, to make one long wing. Pop the balloon and make slits in the shell on either side in the middle and towards the back. Push the wing through the middle slit, and another ice cream stick through the end slit to form the tail.

4

Push a craft stick into the front end of the doodlebug, leaving about 2cm sticking out.

5

Cut two short pieces, 2cm high, from the cardboard tube. Glue them to the top of the doodlebug, one above the wings and one above the tail. Cut another piece of tube about 10cm long, and glue it across the short pieces.

6

Paint the doodlebug with grey acrylic paint.

Did you know...
The months from June to August 1944 became known as the 'Doodlebug Summer'.

make an
Anderson shelter

During air raids, people had to shelter from bombs in public shelters such as the London Underground tunnels, or in shelters they had set up indoors or in their gardens. The outdoor shelters were called Anderson shelters and were made from corrugated iron.

You will need:

- ◎ Corrugated card
- ◎ Shoe box lid
- ◎ Scissors
- ◎ Glue
- ◎ Green card
- ◎ Silver metallic paint
- ◎ Brushes
- ◎ Tissue paper
- ◎ Kitchen scouring pads
- ◎ Dry used tea bags

1 Cut a piece of corrugated card, bend it into an arc shape with the ridges showing and glue the edges inside the shoe box lid.

2 Cut two pieces of corrugated card to form the ends. Cut away a rectangle at one end to make a door. Glue both ends onto the arc with the corrugated ridges showing.

3

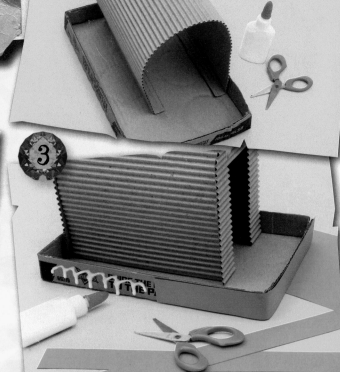

Cut strips of green card, and use them to cover the edges of the shoe box lid.

4 Paint the cardboard using silver metallic paint.

5 Fill the space around the shelter with tissue paper, and stick scouring pads on top.

6 Make small piles of dry used tea bags to look like sandbags around the shelter door.

Did you know...
Indoor 'Morrison' shelters were cage shelters that could also be used as tables.

make a
Wireless set

There was no television during World War II, but most homes had a radio set called a wireless. Families would gather round it to hear news about the war, or listen to their favourite radio programmes, jazz or big band music.

1 Draw the dial and the speaker shape onto one side of the box and cut them out.

2 Cut a piece of gold netting larger than the speaker cut-out. Glue it in place on the inside of the box. Cut a ring of gold card and glue it around the edges of the dial cut-out.

3 Cut a piece of card the same size as the dial hole. Draw the dial marks and numbers in marker pen, and then cut out a piece of cellophane big enough to cover the dial face.

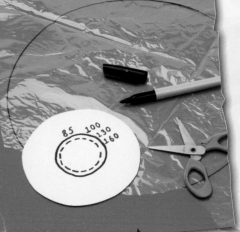

85 100 130 160

4 Glue the cellophane circle onto the card dial, then glue the card inside the box so the dial face shows through the hole. Cut out dial hands from the gold card, and glue them onto the cellophane.

5 Cut small circles of gold card and glue them either side of the dial. Paint two bottle tops black and glue them onto the gold circles.

Did you know...
Radio broadcasts by the Prime Minister Winston Churchill helped to keep people's spirits up.

6 Paint the box brown, using a darker shade to suggest wood markings.

make a
Spitfire aeroplane

During the Battle of Britain in 1940, British and German fighter planes fought to gain control of the skies over Britain. British MK1 spitfire planes became a familiar sight. Single-seat planes carrying four pairs of machine guns, they were famously powerful, light and aerodynamic in design.

1 Copy the templates at the back of the book onto the card. Colour in the markings on the wings, body and tail.

2 Cut the pieces out, then fold and glue the two wing halves together.

3 Glue the two sides of the plane body together except for the flaps at the bottom and the tip of the nose. Fold the flaps at the bottom back, and glue them to the wings so the green markings face upwards.

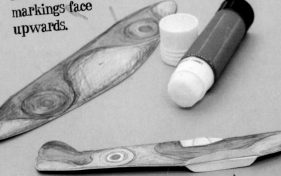

4 Fold and glue the two rudder halves. Cut a slit in the rudder and a slit in the tail and push the rudder into the tail.

5 Glue the propeller to the nose.

Did you know...
The Battle of Britain was fought to control the skies over Britain in the summer of 1940.

make
Pilots' goggles

During the war, Royal Air Force (RAF) pilots flew fighter and bomber planes to attack the enemy. They wore goggles to keep the wind, dirt and bugs out of their eyes as they sat in open cockpits without roofs.

1 Glue two sheets of craft foam together. The piece should be about the width of your forehead. To make it look like leather, sponge on black paint then sponge over it using brown paint.

2 Cut out a mask shape then draw around the plastic lids to mark where the lenses will go. Cut out circles slightly smaller than the marked lines.

3 Cover the rims of the lids with black gaffa tape.

4 Stick the lids to the front of the goggles, making sure they cover the holes.

5 Cut small slits on either side of the mask.

6 Cut a piece of black elastic that will stretch to fit around the back of your head. Thread the ends through the slits and knot or secure them at the back.

Did you know...
Pilots' flying suits were lined with wool for warmth. Some had electric wires to warm up gloves and boots.

make a
Draught-stopper

During the war, a government campaign encouraged families to 'make do and mend'. Newspapers and women's magazines carried ideas for recyling materials, such as old clothes or curtains.

1 Cut off one of the trouser legs.

2 Turn the trouser leg inside out and stitch up one end.

3 Fill the trouser leg with rice or cushion stuffing and stitch up the other end.

4

Cut out decorative shapes from the fabric scraps.

5

Stick the shapes onto the draught-stopper with fabric glue.

6

Make a tassle from ribbon and leftover fabric and glue or stitch it to the draught-stopper.

Did you know...
Few homes in the 1940s had central heating. Most had open fires but coal was hard to get.

make

Decoy sneakers

During the war, spies were sent on secret operations to enemy countries. Spies landing on beaches in Asia and the Pacific region wore decoy sneakers so that they could go onshore without being detected. These were rubber overshoes that left footprints like the bare feet of local people.

1 Stand on the card in bare feet. Draw around your feet and your toes, drawing in between your big toe and second toe.

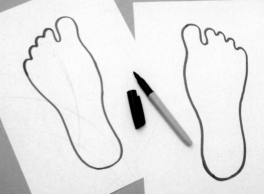

2 Draw around the outline again leaving a margin to make a larger footprint, then cut around the outer line.

3 Stick two sheets of craft foam together and, using the card templates, cut out two footprints.

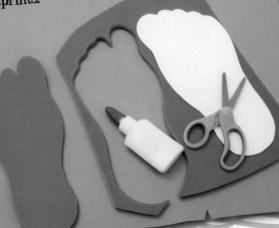

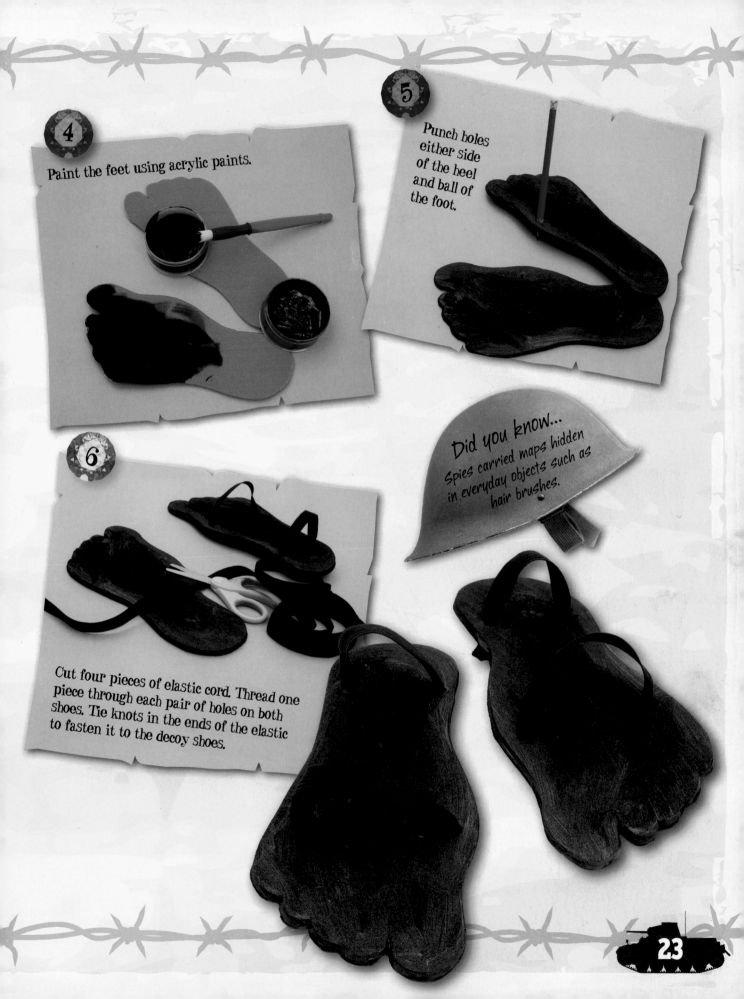

4

Paint the feet using acrylic paints.

5

Punch holes either side of the heel and ball of the foot.

6

Cut four pieces of elastic cord. Thread one piece through each pair of holes on both shoes. Tie knots in the ends of the elastic to fasten it to the decoy shoes.

Did you know...
Spies carried maps hidden in everyday objects such as hair brushes.

make an Evacuee's suitcase

Nearly two million children were evacuated from London and other cities to escape the bomb raids. Some were sent by ship to live overseas. Others travelled by train to the countryside, carrying a few belongings in a small leather suitcase labelled with their name.

1 Crumple up the brown paper several times to crease it all over then smooth it out and paint white glue onto the smooth side. Leave to dry, crumple it again, and then flatten it.

2 Cover both cereal boxes with the brown paper, and glue or tape it in place.

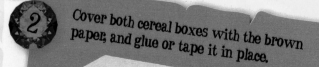

3 Glue one box on top of the other, with the thinner box on top.

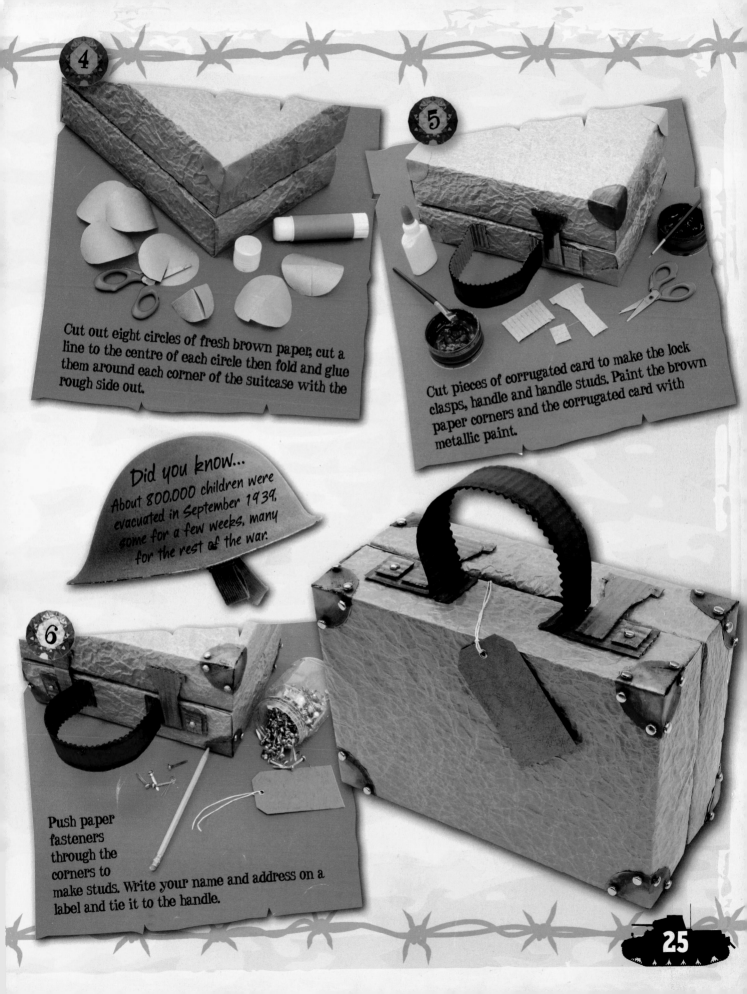

4

Cut out eight circles of fresh brown paper, cut a line to the centre of each circle then fold and glue them around each corner of the suitcase with the rough side out.

5

Cut pieces of corrugated card to make the lock clasps, handle and handle studs. Paint the brown paper corners and the corrugated card with metallic paint.

Did you know...
About 800,000 children were evacuated in September 1939, some for a few weeks, many for the rest of the war.

6

Push paper fasteners through the corners to make studs. Write your name and address on a label and tie it to the handle.

make War medals

War medals were awarded to servicemen and women for service to their country. The colours of ribbons stood for the Army, Marines and Air Force, and special medals or stars were awarded for service in different countries and campaigns.

Draw two identical squares onto graph paper. Divide one into 16 squares and draw a circle inside it. Divide the other into 64 squares and draw a star inside it. Cut out the circle and the star.

2 Using the paper shapes as templates, cut out gold stars and silver circles from the card.

3 Tape a paper clip vertically onto the back of half of the stars and half of the circles.

4

Glue circles and stars with paper clips to circles and stars without paper clips.

5

Cut 18cm lengths of duct tape and stick red, white and blue ribbons onto them, arranging them in stripes. Fold in the ends, then fold the ribbons in half and stick them to the paper clips.

Did you know...
Medals were also awarded to civilians for bravery or 'gallantry'.

6

Use glitter glue to mark in the letters GRI VI (for King George VI) and a crown above them on the stars, and the King's head on the silver medal.

make a
Victory Day souvenir

The war ended in Europe when Germany surrendered on 8th May 1945. People held parties to celebrate, decorating streets and homes with bunting, flags and badges in the colours of the Union Jack and the British forces.

1 Take a piece of clay and work it with your hands to soften it. Roll it out flat.

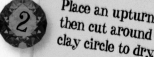

2 Place an upturned plate or bowl onto the clay, then cut around it using a clay tool. Allow the clay circle to dry.

3 Draw a V shape and a circle onto the clay. Draw the banner and the outlines of an aeroplane, a ship and a tank.

Paint the letter V and the aeroplane dark blue. Paint the triangle, circle, ship and tank light blue. It might need two or three layers of paint.

Paint a small red circle, leaving a white space between the red and light blue circles and paint the banner red.

6

Use a marker pen to write 'Victory Day souvenir' in capital letters on the banner, and to go around the detail of the souvenir.

Did you know...
The war in the Pacific region ended with the surrender of Japan on 14th August, 1945.

Glossary

Aerodynamic Smooth and streamlined in shape, so that air can pass freely over and around.

Air raid An attack by enemy aircraft.

Ally A friendly country, or one that helps another country in times of trouble or war.

ARP warden An official appointed to organize people during air raids and blackouts.

Battle of Britain A battle fought between British and German aircraft in late 1940.

Blackout The wartime ban on all lighting, including street and house lights.

Blockade Blocking an area with ships or soldiers to prevent goods and people from going in or out.

Bomber An aeroplane designed to drop bombs.

Bunting A row of cloth or paper flags on a string.

Civilian A member of the public who is not in the military or the police service.

Cockpit The part of an aircraft where the pilot sits.

Corrugated iron A sheet of iron that has been bent into a wavy shape to strengthen it.

Decoy Something used to fool someone or somebody.

Evacuate To send someone (known as an evacuee) away from an area of danger to a safe place.

Goggles Protective glasses with edges that fit closely against the face.

Home Front The name given to what was happening in Britain whilst the war was being fought.

Overshoes Shoes that are designed to be worn over another pair of shoes.

Pacific In, or relating to, the Pacific Ocean.

Ration To limit supplies of goods such as food, clothes and petrol because of shortages.

Recycling Re-using something old.

Serviceman/woman A man or woman who is a member of the armed forces.

Siren A machine used for sounding an air-raid warning.

Spy A person employed by a government to gather information about another country in secret.

Surrender To stop fighting and admit defeat.

Further information

BOOKS

History On Your Doorstep: World War II Britain by Stewart Ross (Franklin Watts, 2012)

Horrible Histories: The Woeful Second World War by Terry Deary (Scholastic, 2007)

Machines That Won the War: World War II by Charlie Samuels (Wayland, 2013)

Men, Women and Children: In the Second World War by Peter Hepplewhite (Wayland, 2012)

What They Don't Tell You About: World War II by Bob Fowke (Wayland, 2013)

World War II Sourcebook: Home Front by Charlie Samuels (Wayland, 2013)

WEBSITES

http://www.bbc.co.uk/schools/primaryhistory/world_war2/
The BBC's website on World War II includes a useful timeline and teacher's notes.

http://www.nationalarchives.gov.uk/education/worldwar2/
This brilliant website from The National Archives contains animated maps and original documents and photographs from World War II.

http://homeworkhelp.stjohnssevenoaks.com/Britain.html
This website is crammed full of facts and interesting information about World War II.

http://www.iwm.org.uk/
Visit the Imperial War Museum's website for information about what life was like for British civilians and soldiers during World War II.

Index

Templates

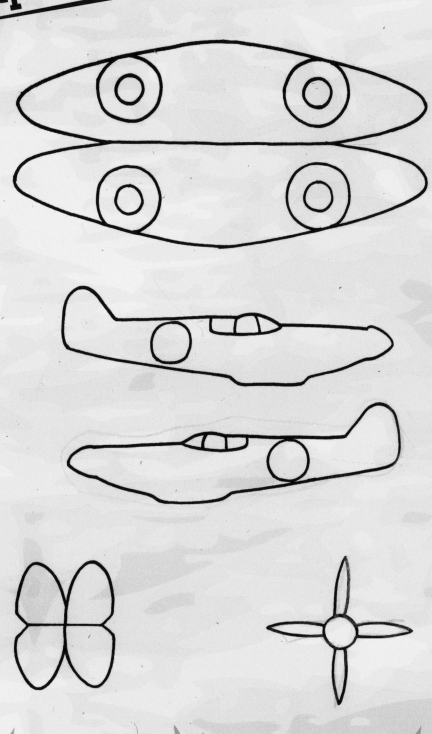